SCOTLAND IN EUROPE

Also by Paul H. Scott:
1707: The Union of Scotland and England (1979)
Walter Scott and Scotland (1981)
John Galt (1985)
In Bed with an Elephant (1985)
The Thinking Nation (1989)
Cultural Independence (1989)
Towards Independence: Essays on Scotland (1991)
Andrew Fletcher and the Treaty of Union (1992)

Edited:
(with A.C. Davis) *The Age of MacDiarmid* (1980)
Sir Walter Scott's *The Letters of Malachi Malagrowther* (1981)
Andrew Fletcher's *United and Separate Parliaments* (1982)
(with George Bruce) *A Scottish Postbag* (1986)
(with A.C. Davis) *Policy for the Arts: A Selection of AdCAS Papers* (1991)

Contributions to joint volumes in:
(ed. J.H. Alexander and David Hewitt) *Scott and his Influence* (1983)
(ed. M. Anderson and L. Dominguez) *Cultural Policy in Europe* (1984)
(ed. Douglas Gifford) *The History of Scottish Literature*, vol. 3 (1988)
(ed. Angus Calder) *Byron and Scotland* (1989)
(ed. C.J.M. MacLachlan and D.S. Robb) *Edwin Muir: Centenary Assessments* (1990)

SCOTLAND IN EUROPE

DIALOGUE WITH A
SCEPTICAL FRIEND

Paul H. Scott

CANONGATE PRESS

First published in 1992 by
Canongate Press plc,
14 Frederick Street,
Edinburgh EH2 2HB.

ISBN 0 86241 414 8

British Library Cataloguing-in-Publication Data
A catalogue record for this book is available on request from
the British Library.

Printed and bound in Scotland by
Bell and Bain Ltd., Glasgow

CONTENTS

As long as but a hundred of us remain alive, never will we on any condition be brought under English rule. It is in truth not for glory, nor riches, nor honours that we are fighting, but for freedom — for that alone, which no honest man gives up but with life itself.

The Declaration of Arbroath (1320)

The miserable and languishing condition of all places that depend upon a remote seat of government.

Andrew Fletcher of Saltoun,
An Account of a Conversation (1704)

Alas, have I often said to myself, what are all the boasted advantages which my country reaps from a certain Union, that can counterbalance the annihilation of her independence, and even her very name?

Robert Burns,
Letter to Mrs Dunlop (1790)

There has been in England a gradual and progressive system of assuming the management of affairs entirely and exclusively proper to Scotland, as if we were totally unworthy of having the management of our own concerns. All must centre in London . . . What are we esteemed by the English? Wretched drivellers, incapable of understanding our own affairs; or greedy speculators, unfit to be trusted? On what ground are we considered either as one or the other?

Sir Walter Scott,
The Letters of Malachi Malagrowther (1826)

By reason of its association with England, Scotland became insular. Its political frontier was broken down, and its mind was walled up. Geographical or political enlargement, beyond certain limits, is nearly always accompanied by intellectual shrinkage.

Eric Linklater,
The Lion and the Unicorn (1935)

If Scots have a long history of being against the government, it isn't surprising. The government was never theirs. That was the shattering result of 1707: the majority of the Scottish people were disenfranchised from their potential rights. They have not yet won them back.

William McIlvanney,
Surviving the Shipwreck (1991)

PREFACE

As this book goes to press, preparations are far advanced for the European Summit in December 1992 in Edinburgh. It is a revolutionary departure for a British government to confer such a distinction on the capital of Scotland, and it is a response to the demand for a Scottish parliament. John Major has said, as if it were a new discovery, that Edinburgh is a capital city and 'a capital city should be the seat of great events'.[1] It has taken many years of pressure for self-government to bring a British government to this conclusion. They are trying the experiment in the hope that it will somehow remove the pressure by persuading us that the British state is not as arrogant, insensitive and remote as it usually seems to us.

The idea that we can be so easily persuaded shows how little they understand the Scottish point of view. They see this attention to Scotland as a flattering gesture; to many of us it is more like a provocation. Scotland is one of the oldest nations in Europe and the first to assert the concept of national self-determination. For centuries we benefited from a close association with other countries in Europe and made important contributions to the development of many of them. It is increasingly intolerable that Scotland should be treated like a province with no right of participation in international affairs. The summit is happening in Edinburgh, but the Scots will be silent spectators, looking through the windows from the outside. John Major wants to widen the Community by admitting many new members, but not Scotland. He is in favour of the doctrine of subsidiarity, that decisions should be taken at the lowest practicable level, but Scotland is excluded. Under these circumstances, the summit in Edinburgh is not a tribute to the nationhood of Scotland, but the flaunting of alien authority.

In the weeks before the General Election on 9 April 1992 English Conservative ministers, who usually do not take much interest in Scotland, descended on us in droves. They were clearly afraid of the SNP because their main concern was to try to persuade the Scots that the Union had 'served us well' and that its dissolution would be disastrous. The Prime Minister, John Major, said that it was a question which transcended the whole election. In a speech in Glasgow on 22 February he conceded that 'no nation can be held irrevocably in a union against its will ... a solitary Scotland means a solitary England, along with Wales and Northern Ireland. Two proud nations. Divorced. Marginalised. Diminished. In place of Great Britain, a little Scotland and a lesser Union — each striving, and not always succeeding, to be heard'.

This was the tone and level of all of these ministerial speeches: a string of extravagant, even hysterical, assertions in emotive language and without supporting evidence or argument. They were reminiscent of the scare propaganda of the 'No' campaign in the referendum of 1979. Once again, they were appealing, not to reason, but to the instinctive fear of radical change and to the feelings of inferiority and insecurity which are the consequence of nearly three centuries of subordination. The sense of *déjà vu* for those who remembered 1979 was increased by the spectacle of the same old war horses, like Lord Weir, trotting out with the same old slogans. Margaret Thatcher during a visit to Scotland showed that she understood the tactic by implying that the Scots would once again take fright.

It is difficult to judge how successful this Conservative tactic was in practice. Their vote rose by only 1.7% over their calamitous result in 1987, but the SNP vote rose by 7.5%. The Conservatives have been able to persuade themselves that it was a victory, partly because they stayed in power as a result of their vote in England, and also because their vote in Scotland, although very poor for a party in government, was better, and that for the SNP worse, than the general expectation. The fact is that the small rise in the Conservative vote can easily be the result of such factors as their lavish expenditure on telephone canvassing, the increase in English residents and the disappearance of many people from the electoral roll because of the Poll Tax.

The Conservative attack had been directed against the Labour and Liberal Democrat, or Constitutional Convention, devolution proposal for a Scottish Parliament with limited powers within the United Kingdom as much as, or sometimes even more than, against independence. Allan Stewart, a minister in the Scottish Office, for instance, has often said that he would prefer independence to devolution, which he thinks is unworkable and a recipe for conflict and confusion. In fact, the Conservatives argued it both ways. When they thought it suited them, they claimed to be the only party which supported the Union. In a speech on 29 November 1991, Ian Lang, the Secretary of State for Scotland, said that power devolved is power retained, but that Labour and the Liberal Democrats went well beyond that in talking of a Scottish parliament and Home Rule: 'What they plan would be a massive breach in the Union of the United Kingdom'.[2] On the other hand, the Conservatives are also quite capable of counting Labour and Liberal votes as votes for the Union, as the same Ian Lang admitted in the Usher Hall debate in January 1992.

It is true that supporters of the Convention scheme have often claimed that their objective is to preserve the Union, although in a modified form, and they propose that many of the most important functions of government (defence, foreign affairs, social security and macro-economic policy) would stay at Westminster. You can therefore add Conservative, Labour and Liberal Democrat votes together and

claim that 77.8% of the voters were in favour of keeping the
Union in some form, even if the Conservatives said the
opposite during the election campaign. On the other hand,
since all the parties other than the Conservatives were in
favour of a Scottish parliament, you can add all these votes
together and conclude that 74.3% were in favour of a
Scottish parliament and at least a degree of autonomy. This
is in line with every opinion poll on the subject for about the
last twenty years. Opinion has fluctuated between devolution and independence, but the two together have invari-
ably shown support for a Scottish parliament at between 70
and 80%. The fact is that Labour, firmly committed to a
Scottish parliament, were once again the clear winners of
the election in Scotland with 39% of the vote and 49 of the
72 seats. You might not think so in the light of their
subsequent conduct, but that is another story.

The small rise in the Conservative vote, after all the
emphasis which they had placed on the constitutional issue,
therefore suggests that they failed to make any substantial
impact on the demand for some form of Scottish parliament. What was the effect on support for independence? An
opinion poll in January had shown this at 50%. Had it
diminished to the 21.5% which the SNP polled in the
election in April? There is no clear answer. Polls have often
shown support for independence at a higher level than
support for the SNP. In an election people vote for a diversity of reasons apart from their views on the constitutional
question. As opinion polls have consistently shown, many
voters for other parties favour independence. In this particular General Election, it was not unreasonable to suppose
that the quickest way to secure constitutional change was
through a vote for Labour. The apparently close contest in
England between the Conservatives and Labour tended to
polarise the vote between them towards the end of the
campaign.

During the election campaign I canvassed in one of the

few comparatively safe Conservative seats in Scotland. I found that many of the scare stories from the ministerial speeches were being played back to me. To some extent, this was a surprise. In spite of what John Major seems to think, this is a debate which has been exhaustively conducted in Scotland for decades. Many of these old stories are obviously absurd; all of them have been repeatedly answered and refuted. We tended to assume that no one was likely to be deceived by such nonsense and that it was better to campaign positively than waste time in endless repetition of old arguments. This was probably a mistake. To many people, the old arguments are not as familiar as we suppose. The debate has been carried on largely in the serious Scottish press and in the Scottish political programmes on radio and television. All of these reach only a minority of the population. Many people read London newspapers and take most of their political information from network television which hardly mentions Scottish issues. In the clamour of an election campaign they are suddenly deluged with conflicting statements. It is not surprising that they should be confused by the complexities of an argument of which they have heard little or that they should be alarmed by frightening talk which come from an apparently authoritative source. The natural reaction is to cling to the illusory security of the *status quo*. The alarmist propaganda has been carefully designed to have precisely that effect.

This experience has led me to have a new look at the case for an independent Scotland within the European Community. The account which follows is a digest of many conversations with people who are reasonably open-minded but sceptical or worried. I have combined their questions and remarks under the initials 'SF' for 'sceptical friend' and the replies under my own.

P.H.S.
Edinburgh
August 1992

P.S. When I finished writing this book in August I did not know that the credibility of the Major government would be undermined, and the vulnerability of the British economy exposed, so dramatically and so soon. Their pretensions to leadership in Europe were never very substantial and they are now threadbare indeed. There could hardly have been a more convincing demonstration of the need for Scottish independence.

After the French referendum there is still uncertainty over the Maastricht Treaty, but there is little doubt that the European Community will continue to expand and develop. In Scotland we want to contribute to this process and ensure that our opinions and interests are taken into account. We can only do this as a member state.

All of these recent events have reinforced the argument which is presented in this dialogue.

P.H.S.
21 September 1992

1. WHY INDEPENDENCE?

SF Can we begin with the obvious first question: why do you think that Scotland should be independent?

PHS I am not sure that it is an obvious question. Did anyone think it necessary to ask why Canada, Australia, New Zealand, Ireland or India wanted independence, or Norway in 1905, the scores of British colonies after the last World War, or more recently the constituent parts of the Soviet Union or Yugoslavia? Do we not find all these cases so natural that we do not have to ask? Suppressed or submerged nations, or dependent territories that have acquired an identity, always want to govern themselves. That is something which we all understand and respect. It is the principle of self-determination which is endorsed by the Charter of the United Nations and many treaties and which virtually all governments have frequently asserted as a basic rule of international relations. Possibly the idea first appeared in Scotland, since the Declaration of Arbroath of 1320 may be the earliest, as well as one of the most eloquent, statements of it.

Even John Major accepts that Scotland is a nation with a long and distinguished history, a 'proud nation',[3] as he has called it. Well, nations with any self-respect always want to take responsibility for their own government. That is all we are asking for, no more and no less, a return to normality.

SF I do not suppose that anyone nowadays would seriously dispute that Scotland has every right to independence, if a majority of the people show that that is what they want. In fact, there is no argument about that because the opponents of constitutional change, including many ministers of the present Conservative government, have conceded the point. The argument is not about the principle, but about the practical consequences in this particular case. What advantages do you see in independence?

PHS In the first place it would be more democratic because we should have the government which we elected, not the one elected by our larger neighbour to the south. It would therefore be a government responsive to our needs and wishes and which can give its first attention to our conditions and problems, not the very different ones to which a British government must give priority. At present we are still, as Jonathan Swift described the Irish in the 18th century, 'patients who have physic sent them by doctors at a distance, strangers to their constitution, and the nature of their disease'.[4] In Scotland still, as in Ireland then, we are expected to obey laws to which we have not given consent and which may violate our sense of social justice or harm our interests. We are administered by the civil servants of the Scottish Office, but they are subject to ministers appointed by the government in London which makes the major decisions of policy. Scotland is unique in the western world, and uniquely undemocratic, as a country with a legal system and a bureaucracy, but no parliament of its own.

This has bad economic, as well as social, consequences. Economic and financial policy is made in London to suit English conditions, but this can be entirely inappropriate for Scotland. The economy in England may be overheating and require restraint at a time when Scotland needs the opposite. Similar consequences follow when the private sector works on a British scale. Decisions made on this basis to move management or manufacturing capacity to England may make sense in that context, but they contribute to the industrial decline of Scotland. The most conspicuous example recently has been in the steel industry, but there have been hundreds of other cases. Scotland without its own parliament and government has been defenceless. In the course of this century a 'self-confident, locally controlled economy' has declined into 'a weakened, externally dependent one'.[5] By the early 1990s only five of the top fifty manufacturing companies were controlled from Scotland. The *Financial Times* on 3 August 1992 reported a survey of British companies which showed that only 4.1% by number and 3.3% by value had their headquarters in Scotland; 58.5% by number and 81% by value had had their headquarters in London and the South East of England. Nothing could illustrate more convincingly the real cost of the Union to Scotland. No independent Scottish government could have tolerated such a decline, nor the steady loss of population through people forced to emigrate to find work.

The takeover of Scottish industry would be bad enough if the british economy was successful. In fact, it has been obvious for a very long time that it is fundamentally unsound and subject to repeated crisis and decline. The collapse of economic policy and yet another devaluation of the pound in September 1992 was only the latest in a long line of disasters under both Conservative and Labour governments. Involvement with such an economy can only be of disadvantage to Scotland.

It is true that major economic and financial decisions are now taken increasingly through the institutions of the European Community. This makes independence still more necessary because we need our own voice in the Community. We should then participate in the decision-making and be able to ensure that account is taken of our interests. National governments will still have an important role for at least the foreseeable future. But as long as the Union continues, Scotland is a mere province with no international existence, no right to belong to international organisations and no right to be heard.

Then there is an important cultural need for independence. We have a valuable and distinctive cultural identity which is worth preserving and developing as part of the diversity which makes the cultural vitality of Europe. Scotland has been closely involved in that diversity for centuries and especially before the Union. The inevitable tendency of the Union is to exercise pressure towards conformity with English standards in language, taste, values and ideas. For this reason *A Claim of Right for Scotland* of 1988 was right in saying that 'the Union has always been, and remains, a threat to the survival of a distinctive culture in Scotland'.[6] In spite of this our culture has more than once recovered from provincial mediocrity, usually in periods of political revival. Independence, as elsewhere, would be likely to give a powerful stimulus to our cultural self-confidence and achievement.

As part of our cultural identity we have our own strong traditions on questions of law, social justice and morality. At present we have no power to amend our laws in accordance with our own views. More often than not, British legislation is applied to Scotland by means of a few clauses cobbled on at the end. This is unsatisfactory and destructive of the intellectual coherence of Scots law. We need our own parliament to provide adequately for the amendment of our laws to meet changing ideas and circumstances.

The psychological need for independence is perhaps the most important of all. As Eric Linklater said, 'people degenerate when they lose control of their own affairs'.[7] Our political impotence under the Union breeds a sense of hopelessness and inferiority, a feeling that everything that really matters happens somewhere else and that you have to leave Scotland to succeed. Independence would give us responsibility and new opportunities. We should have no one to blame but ourselves, but a chance to make Scotland a better place. Everywhere in the world where countries have achieved or recovered independence, there has been an upsurge of self-confidence, optimism and social and economic progress. I have no doubt that independence would bring the same transformation to Scotland.

SF   I can see that this is a strong case, but what about the argument that a Scottish parliament would inevitably be dominated by the Labour Party and the central belt?

PHS   This is, of course, one of the old scare stories. It is based on the distortions of the 'first past the post' electoral system where a party with less than a majority of the votes quite often wins a large majority of the seats. The Labour Party, with most of its support in the central belt, has done this in the last four elections. All of the proposals for a Scottish parliament, however, envisage proportional representation. This would prevent any such distortion; all parties would have a share of the seats which reflects their support all over the country. Quite apart from that, any Scottish parliament, depending on Scottish votes alone, is likely to have more regard and understanding for the needs and wishes of all parts of Scotland than a British parliament which has to respond to a different electorate.

SF   Even so, is Scotland really so badly off under the present system? Allan Massie in a recent newspaper article said that it was quite untrue that Scotland was a poor and wretched country: 'It is a reasonably prosperous and reasonably happy part of an unusually fortunate part of the world'.[8] Is there not some truth in that?

PHS   Yes, of course. We are not arguing for independence because Scotland is an extreme case of misery and suppression, but because it falls so far short of its potential. Compare Scotland to the smaller independent countries of western Europe which are about our size, countries such as Norway, the Netherlands, Denmark, Switzerland or Austria. What do you find? Most of them are far poorer in natural resources than Scotland, but they are far ahead of us by almost any standard of measurement in prosperity and quality of life. Their wealth per head is greater and they have better health services, education and pensions. Not surprisingly, they radiate an air of satisfaction and optimism which is very different from the resigned despair to which so many of our people have been reduced. It is difficult to think of any reason for this contrast except that they have their own government to look after their interests and we do not. The independent part of Ireland achieved its independence when it had a far weaker economy than Scotland, and that was largely due to the centuries of misrule from London. Since independence, and particularly since they became a member state of the European Community, the Irish have made great progress.

Also, Allan Massie's comment would seem unbearably complacent and uninformed to people who are unemployed and living in Easterhouse or Craigmillar or, even worse, are homeless. Scotland is comfortable enough if you have a job or an income of some kind; but we have shameful levels of poor housing, unemployment, poverty and ill-health. Much of this is the consequence of years of government which is irresponsible in both senses of the word. We are unlikely to see a determined effort to solve the problems which surround us in Scotland until we have a government which we elect and which cannot escape responsibility by blaming someone else. We must find our own solutions.

There is another consequence of our lack of control over our own affairs. Whether we like it or not, we have nuclear submarines based on the Clyde. Nuclear waste, which other governments do not want on their own territory, is sent to Dounreay for reprocessing and crosses the rest of Scotland on the way. Also, the land of Scotland can be bought and sold by anyone and misused or neglected as they please. Independent countries can refuse to accept nuclear weapons, or noxious waste from other people, and exercise some control over the way in which land is sold and used. In these, as in other, aspects, Scotland is singularly vulnerable and defenceless.

SF   I suppose that some people would argue that nuclear weapons are necessary for defence in an uncertain world. If that is true, then it would be an argument which every government in the world could use, and we could have nuclear proliferation on a hideous scale. But I agree with you on this one. I think nuclear weapons were never a protection but an invitation to nuclear destruction. Any case that might have been made for them in the past has now disappeared along with the Soviet threat. I suppose that the only explanation of the British addiction to nuclear weapons is the British, or perhaps rather the English, desire to cling to the remnants of their former status as what used to be called a Great Power.

To come back to the constitutional point, is there not another British myth, that their parliamentary system has unique virtues and that Scotland is fortunate to be able to share in it? This notion was reflected in a letter which the former Conservative Prime Minister, Lord Home of the Hirsel, sent recently to the *Scotsman*.[9] He said that the partnership between Scotland and England had won 'huge prizes', firstly British parliamentary democracy and secondly the Commonwealth, and implied that because of that we should stay with the Union. Is this an argument that carries any weight?

PHS   I do not think that it is so much an argument as an appeal to sentiment. Through our schools, the monarchy, the BBC and all the rest of it, we are brought up under a great pressure of British sentiment. The Unionists are weak on rational argument, but strong on efforts to stir up barely conscious feelings. No doubt the effect is to encourage people to cling to the *status quo*, and that has effects on the way they vote, as long as they do not think about it very seriously.

Even if the British parliamentary system and the Commonwealth were as splendid as Lord Home would have us believe, that is not a reason why we should not have our own parliament. In fact, Scottish independence is consistent with the whole ethos of the Commonwealth, which was created by the evolution of dependent territories towards self-government. Scotland would be following the example of Canada and all the rest.

As for the British parliamentary system, it is hardly an example that anyone would want to follow. It gives almost unlimited power, and vast patronage, to a Prime Minister. The electoral system distorts the will of the electorate. There is no written constitution, no guarantee of human rights and no freedom of information. The working hours, the fancy dress and the mumbo-jumbo are absurd. In the days of arbitrary monarchs in other countries, this system was an admirable curb on royal power. Now it is partly a picturesque relic and partly a form of elective dictatorship. It is more a model of what to avoid than an inspiration to follow. A Scottish parliament would benefit from the example of Westminster by avoiding its absurdities and excesses.

2. HAS THE UNION
'SERVED SCOTLAND WELL'?

SF We have just been discussing a Conservative appeal to the past in defence of the Union. Another phrase which they use very often is: the Union has 'served Scotland well'. Has it, in fact?

PHS I notice that they always put this in the past tense and take it as so axiomatic that it needs no supporting evidence. This is a relic of attitudes which were prevalent in the 19th century and have lingered on in some school textbooks and other places. In fact, the consequences of the Union have been different at different times and the answer to this question depends on the period under discussion. We therefore have to look at it historically.

The English government wanted an incorporating union in 1707 for political and strategic reasons; they wanted to make it impossible for an independent Scotland to become once again a threat on their northern border in alliance with a country with which England might be at war. All sides admitted at the time that the great majority of the Scottish people were thoroughly opposed to the loss of independence. The Scottish parliament, like all others at that time, represented only a minute proportion of the population. Its members acquiesced in the Union, partly because of bribery and other appeals to their self-interest, and partly because of a fear that the alternative was invasion by England and the imposition of worse terms.

It is, by the way, untrue that the Union was a bargain in which the Scots exchanged their independence for trading concessions and access to the English and colonial market.

This was a rationalisation thought up in the 19th century to try to explain why a country, which had defended its independence against heavy odds for hundreds of years, seemed suddenly to capitulate so easily. At the time Scottish trading interests petitioned against the Union precisely because they realised that manufacturers in Scotland would be overwhelmed by imports from England and that Scottish trade would be damaged by English duties and regulations designed for English conditions. They were absolutely right. The first economic effects of the Union were disastrous for Scotland. It took about fifty years before Scotland began to recover through its own efforts, and through new agricultural and industrial technology, much of it due to Scottish inventions. The age of steam owes much to James Watt, just as the electronic present does to Clerk Maxwell.

The Union extinguished the Scottish (and in theory also the English) parliaments, but it left most of the other institutions intact, including the Church of Scotland, the legal system, education and local administration. At that time central governments did very little anywhere in the world, except make war and levy taxes to pay for them. Having successfully reduced Scotland to impotence as a possible trading or political rival, Westminster took very little further interest in our affairs. The only exception during the rest of the century was the ruthless suppression of the Highlands after the '45 and the virtual destruction of their way of life. Apart from that, Scotland was left, as Walter Scott said, 'under the guardianship of her own institutions, to win her silent way to national wealth and consequence'.[10]

This began to change early in the 19th century. The demands of the Napoleonic Wars, English self-confidence after the victory of Waterloo, improved communications with steamships and steam trains, all led Westminster to take a more active role and to intervene increasingly in Scottish affairs. The first notable protest against this, which you might call in fact the first manifesto of modern Scottish nationalism, was the work of Walter Scott which I have just quoted, *The Letters of Malachi Malagrowther* of 1826. 'There has been in England', he wrote, 'a gradual and progressive system of assuming the management of affairs entirely and exclusively proper to Scotland, as if we were totally unworthy of having the management of our own concerns. All must centre in London'.[11] This was a powerful and convincing protest but Scotland was largely defenceless. Only a very small part of the population so far had the vote. Memories of the aftermath of the '45, which had been at least partly a rebellion against the Union, were still fresh.

A new element now entered the equation, the growth of the British Empire as, for a time, the greatest power in the world. The union was a humiliation which had damaged Scottish self-esteem and brought much harm and little good. The Empire, which was seen by many Scots as a successful joint venture with England, became a substitute for national achievement. As Michael Lynch says in his *New History of Scotland,* the Scots embraced not Britain, but the British Empire.[12] It provided careers for individual Scots in the army (to which many literally gave their lives), colonial administration and emigration. Much of Scottish industry, at that time still largely owned and controlled in Scotland, manufactured raw materials from the Empire or built ships and locomotives for the Empire market.

It was during this period of imperial grandeur, of pride in the Empire on which the sun never set, the Union Jack and the map painted red, that the idea that the Union was a self-evident good began to be accepted. Even respectable historians wrote on this assumption, and it found its way into school textbooks and the standard clichés of political speeches and the newspaper leaders. An enormous weight of propaganda was invested in it. It became part of conventional wisdom. That was not unreasonable, if you believed that the Empire was itself desirable, for it probably could not have come about with the Union and certainly Scotland would not have been involved. Now most of us think of the imperial past with more shame than pride, but that was not the prevalent view at the time.

This focus on the Empire meant that Scotland itself was neglected, with no parliament and government of our own to discuss the problems and take decisions. Andrew Fletcher of Saltoun, who was one of the most formidable opponents of the Union in 1707, accurately predicted its outcome. He said that it would lead to the concentration of the wealth of the whole island in the south-east corner of England and the decline of Scotland to 'the miserable and languishing condition of all places that depend on a remote seat of government'. It would be 'like a farm managed by servants, and not under the eye of the master'.[13] The growth of the Empire increased this effect by distracting attention still further from Scotland. Energy and talent was drained away at the expense of Scotland itself.

Towards the end of this period, Edwin Muir, in *Scottish Journey* (1935), said that the result was 'that Scotland is gradually being emptied of its population, its spirit, its wealth, industry, art, intellect, and innate character'. Scotland was falling apart because it had no visible and effective power to hold it together and it needed independence urgently if it was to survive.[14] Even when the Empire was still in its heyday, in the 80s and 90s of the last century, this danger and this need became increasingly apparent and the demand for self-government has been growing ever since.

My conclusion then is that the idea that the Union brought benefits to Scotland is a relic of the imperial past and that it was questionable even then, apart from the moral and other objections to the Empire as the exercise of control over other people.

SF   So you think that the Union is now obsolete and serves no useful purpose?

PHS Exactly. Scotland should have followed the example of Canada and the other former colonies years ago and recovered its independence. But the Union is out of date in other respects as well. The argument which used to be produced in its support was that it gave access to a wider market than Scotland alone. Now, of course, the European Community has widened the market to include almost the whole of western Europe and it is likely to expand still further. The old case for the Union has therefore disappeared completely.

The United Kingdom is also outdated because it is a multi-national state, and a very highly centralised one at that. Almost every other such state has dissolved into its component parts and for good reasons. Multi-national states are resented by the submerged nations who want to control their own affairs and, perhaps partly for this reason, they are cumbersome, inefficient and economically unsuccessful. The decentralised and small and independent states of western Europe are conspicuously more prosperous than the over-centralised UK. In fact, contrary to the prevailing tendency everywhere else, the UK in recent years has been becoming more centralised and not less. This is also in contradiction to the European Community doctrine of susidiarity, which the British government professes to support. According to this, decisions should be taken on the lowest practical level and closest to the people they affect. John Major accepts this idea, but seems to think that it should come to a halt at Westminster. He is right about the letter but not the spirit of the Maastricht Treaty. If he is as enthusiastic about the principle of susidiarity as he pretends, he should welcome its extension to Scotland. Member states should apply within their own territory the same principles which apply between themselves and the Community.

The new Europe which is now emerging is one in which small independent nations, or in some cases decentralised federations but not multi-national conglomerates, co-operate for their mutual advantage. It is significant that a very early advocate of such an arrangement was the same Andrew Fletcher who opposed in the 18th century both the loss of Scottish independence and the domination of Europe by one great power. For centuries before that time Scotland was closely involved in the rest of Europe. We derived much benefit and also contributed substantially to many other countries. To quote Michael Lynch again, the SNP policy of independence in Europe 're-establishes one of the most important threads of continuity in Scottish history'.[15] Scotland could, once again, make a valuable and distinctive contribution.

SF I should like to return to the European aspect in more detail later, but first one or two other points about the real or alleged advantages of the Union within the UK. In the famous Usher Hall debate in January 1992 Ian Lang said: 'Scotland's greatest days have been since the Union. Our greatest economic growth, our cultural flowering, our arts and our heritage come from the last 300 years'.[16] He seems to be implying that these things not only followed the Union, but were a result of it. Is that a fair point?

PHS Certainly not. This remark, I remember, rightly provoked a howl of derision from the audience. This was the right response because Lang was either revealing a complete ignorance of Scottish history or distorting it quite cynically. Unionists often like to suggest that art and civilisation arrived in Scotland with the Union, but this is as nonsensical as it is insulting. Was it a barbarous people who built the border Abbeys and rebuilt them several times when they were destroyed in successive English invasions until their final destruction by the army of Henry VIII? In the Middle Ages and Renaissance we had great poets like Dunbar and Henryson, the outstanding scholar and neo-

classical poet, George Buchanan, philosophers such as
Ireland and Mair whose work prepared the way for the
Scottish Enlightenment, and Napier, the inventor of loga-
rithms. The Scottish contribution to civilisation, then as
later, was remarkable for so small a country and we were in
very close touch with intellectual developments in the rest
of Europe. It is not true that Scotland was a particularly
violent and unruly country in the past; on the contrary, our
record in this respect compares favourably with most other
countries including England.

Unionists sometimes claim the Scottish Enlightenment
of the 18th century as a product of the Union, as if such a
remarkable outburst of intellectual achievement could be
created out of nothing in a couple of generations. In fact, all
serious scholarship on this matter has found its roots deep
in the Scottish past. John MacQueen, for example, has
concluded that 'the Scottish Enlightenment was the natural, almost the inevitable, outcome of several centuries of
Scottish and European intellectual history'.[17]

Of course it is true that the greatest economic growth in
Scotland, as everywhere else, has been in the last 300 years.
As I said before, this was due to new technologies, much of
them invented in Scotland. The Empire connection, while
it lasted, stimulated some sectors of the Scottish economy;
but, as we have seen, this was very much a mixed blessing.
It is impossible to be certain how Scotland would have
developed if we had succeeded in keeping our independence; but a comparison with independent European countries of a similar size suggest that we would now be in a much
more prosperous and satisfactory condition.

SF   But surely we have gained something from our association with England. What about the language of Shake-
speare, their traditions of justice and fairness, institutions
like the BBC and the Health Service?

PHS The English have many admirable qualities and I have no doubt that we have learned many things from them, just as we have from the Italians, French and Dutch and many other peoples and they from us. The English language is now even more useful for international communication than Latin was in the Middle Ages, but it is a pity that we have allowed it to supplant rather than complement our own expressive forms of speech. In matters of law, justice, tolerance and fairness none of us are perfect, but recent experience suggests that Scottish practice is not inferior to the English, to put it mildly. We have our own very valuable traditions on these matters. I suppose that it was the Scot, Lord Reith, who did more than anyone to establish the BBC ethos of public service broadcasting. Its future under a Conservative government is uncertain, but in any case it has spent most of the revenue raised in Scotland on programme making in England. We need an autonomous organisation of our own. The Health Service, too, would probably be safer in Scottish hands.

The economist, E.F. Schumacher, said that it was not necessary for Germany to annex the United States before it could sell Volkswagens there.[18] It is the same with cultural and intellectual influence. We can all learn from other countries without being part of the same state. In fact, it is better not to be part of the same state because we can then pick and choose as we please. As part of the UK we have had to adopt many English practices whether we liked them or not. As an independent country we could exercise freedom of choice in the matter.

This is one of the reasons why independence would greatly improve our relations with England. At present, we have to accept the government chosen by the English electorate and suffer the frustration of seeing our views and aspirations ignored. This is bound to cause tension and resentment. We shall have a much healthier, friendlier and more co-operative relationship when we are both independent partners within the European Community. Relations between Norway and Sweden improved out of all recognition after Norway achieved independence in 1905. So was it also between Britain and her former colonies. So it will be between Scotland and England.

3. SCOTLAND TOO SMALL?

SF What is your reply to the people who argue that Scotland is too small to stand on its own feet as an independent country?

PHS Well, there is a line in one of MacDiarmid's longer poems where he expresses astonishment that the question should be asked: 'Scotland small? Our multiform, our infinite Scotland *small*?'[19] Astonishment is the right reaction because many of the most prosperous, civilised and happy countries in the world are about the same size as Scotland or smaller. An official publication of the European Community arranges the member states in order of prosperity. Taking 100 to represent the average, Luxemburg, with a total population less than that of Edinburgh, is at the top with a score of 140. Germany, which is large but federal, is second with just over 120. Denmark, with a population about the same as Scotland, is third at 120. The UK is sixth with just over 100, slightly ahead of Belgium.[20]

Many countries which have recently become independent, with equal voting rights in the United Nations and a fully recognised international identity, are very much smaller than Scotland. No one has questioned the suitability for independence of Latvia, Lithuania or Estonia, for example, on grounds of size. In fact, I should say that Scotland is about the ideal size for an independent nation. It is large enough to sustain all that a country needs and to contain a variety of character and terrain, but not so large that government becomes remote and impersonal. I have experienced countries of various sizes and my impression is that it is the citizens of the smaller countries, such as Norway, Denmark, Austria or Switzerland, who are the most content.

SF   Are we rich enough?

PHS   Scotland has a developed, industrial economy, and a standard of living which people in many parts of the world would think enviably high. When we have control of our own affairs, we shall have the potential to be very prosperous indeed. We have 80% of Europe's resources in oil and 30% of the fish. We produce more food and energy than we need for own consumption. Not only are we rich in coal, oil and water power, but we are particularly well placed for the sources of energy of the future, wind and tidal power. Our people are talented, resourceful and inventive. Even if our education is not as pre-eminent as it once was, it still produces many well educated minds. When you compare the standard of living which countries like Denmark and Switzerland have been able to maintain with far poorer natural resources, you can have some idea of what an independent Scotland could achieve.

SF   But it is not true that Scotland benefits financially from the Union?

PHS   Just before the last General Election the Scottish Office, evidently ignoring the usual civil service rules about political impartiality, published a booklet[21] about government expenditure and revenue in Scotland. This made the point that Scotland has 8.9% of the population of the UK but receives 10% of 'identifiable' public expenditure. On the revenue side, it had a table showing a decline in the Scottish contribution to income tax from 8.5% in 1978–79 to 7.6% in 1988–89. Without giving a breakdown for other taxes, it said that 'revenues per head in Scotland tend to be slightly lower than the UK average'.

What do these figures prove? The booklet says that more than half of the 'identifiable' expenditure is on social security and health. Now social security payments are an indication of unemployment, and poverty. So, to a large extent, is expenditure on the Health Service because the shockingly bad health statistics in Scotland are related to unemployment and poverty. The decline in our contribution to income tax also reflects a decline in earnings. These figures published by the Government itself are therefore an admission that the Union has failed Scotland by resulting in a lower and declining standard of living than in England. This is astonishing when you consider the oil in Scottish waters and our wealth in natural resources and their high ratio to our population. The figures, whatever the intention behind their publication, are not an argument for the Union but against it.

They are far from the whole story. Corporation tax is levied on companies wherever their head office is. Many of the largest companies trading in Scotland, and making profits from their Scottish customers, have their head offices in London or elsewhere in the south-east of England. That is where the tax on their Scottish profits is paid. Also, 'identifiable' expenditure is a conveniently flexible term. Jim Ross, who retired recently as a senior civil servant in the Scottish Office, has said that 'identifiable' public expenditure happens to be just what the government and treasury choose to make identifiable'.[22] They can therefore adjust it to suit whatever point they are trying to prove.

In fact, the real situation is the precise opposite from the one which the booklet seems to be trying to establish. George Rosie in *Scotching The Myth*[23] has shown that 'non-identified' government expenditure is overwhelmingly directed towards London and the south-east of England in the concentration of government offices, defence procurement, research establishments, mortgage tax relief, transport subsidies, road-building and massive schemes like Docklands and the airports. Andrew Fletcher was right: centres of decision-making attract economic activity and wealth. Impotent provinces tend to decline. That is one of the reasons why Scotland needs independence.

SF How then do you explain that the managing directors of two major insurance companies and of at least one engineering company threatened to remove their head offices from Scotland if that happened?

PHS I agree that this is difficult to understand, unless they were merely coming to the aid of their party by saying something which they thought would be of short-term benefit to the Tories. They used the pretext that many of their customers were in England, but in the Europe of a single market this is absurd. Companies in any country in the Community can do business in any other with complete freedom. Modern communications have eliminated distance and borders. If the attitude of these managing directors is rational, they must have other factors in mind. They may be afraid that the parliament of an independent Scotland would automatically have a Labour majority and would adopt left-wing policies to the detriment of their business interests. As I said before, this ignores the effect of proportional representation which would make any extremist policies unlikely. A Scottish government would stand or fall by its success in improving conditions in Scotland and making it more prosperous. It would want to improve the economy, not make difficulties for it.

Some of these businessmen talk as if an independent Scotland and England would engage in some sort of trade war. This is nonsense. We should still be a valuable market for England as England would be for us. More than that, we should both be part of the infinitely larger market of the European Community and that is committed to interdependence and co-operation.

A man who moves in senior business circles has told me that there is a great deal of simple snobbery and prejudice behind the attitudes of some of them. They have contempt for their fellow Scots. This goes back a long way, of course. As far back as 1603, no less. The royal court was them the source of fashion and prestige. When James VI flitted with his court to London, the process began of the denigration of everything Scottish. English speech, fashion and values became synonymous with wealth and power. The Scots were assumed to be inferior, simply because they were not English, and this was fortified by an ignorance of Scottish history and achievement. If you are infected with this attitude, you might conclude that it is better to be ruled by the English than by your own people.

SF   The Conservatives have made great play of the risk of Scotland becoming the most highly taxed part of the UK and therefore discouraging business and foreign investment.

PHS   This is brass neck from a government under whom business rates in Scotland have for many years been much higher than those in England. We have for years had the experience of higher taxes.

They are talking here about the Labour-Liberal Democrat proposal for devolution, a Scottish parliament of limited power within the UK. They are making a fuss over very little. In this case, taxation would be as in the rest of the UK, apart from a power to make a small variation. In an independent Scotland all taxes would be decided by the Scottish parliament. With the taxation revenues from oil and the savings on Trident submarines and other extravagances, there should be a good possibility of reduced levels of general taxation. We should certainly not want to put ourselves at a disadvantage in relation to our neighbours.

It comes back in the end to Fletcher's point about the farm managed by servants. If we are running our own country, we are likely to make a better job of it than anyone else. Leading economists in the City of London have agreed. Peter Spencer of Shearson Lehman, for instance, has said that independence would enhance the benefits of belonging to the European Community. Scotland would then be likely to have much more support from regional funds, and be able to get a grip on its own industrial problems. Kleinwort Benson have calculated that an independent Scotland, even without taking oil into account, would have a GDP of about the European Community average.[24]

The Scottish steel industry is a good example of the consequences of being an impotent part of a larger unit. Within British Steel it was peripheral and could be starved of investment in favour of concentration further south. As long as Britain was the unit, Scottish steel was only a minor part of a larger whole and it could be sacrificed to rationalise and reduce overall production. If Scotland as a member state of the European Community was the unit, then the prosperity of the Scottish steel industry would have been recognised as an essential national interest.

SF   The end of Ravenscraig is the culmination of the disappearance of Scottish heavy industry, the sad litany of Corpach, Linwood, Bathgate and all the rest of it. Coal and steel used to be major Scottish industries. We used to lead the world in the building of ships and locomotives. Now we have lost so much that I have met people who think that this is a reason why we can no longer hope to stand on our own feet. They say that it is too late.

PHS   I would say rather that it is a proof of the urgent need for us to take responsibility for our own affairs. We still have the infrastructure of an advanced industrial society, even if we badly need to develop direct sea and air links with other countries. Some new industries have taken the place of those we have lost. We are a major oil producer. We export more per head in manufacturing industry than Germany or Japan. We have, by certain measurements, the second largest financial services industry in the whole of the European Community. Scotland is the twenty-third richest country in the world in terms of income per head, on a par with Australia and New Zealand. With our capable population, resources, energy, water and space, we are still in a much more favourable position than most countries in the world to tackle our obvious problems.

SF   Other people have told me, on the contrary, that it is too soon, that Scotland is not yet ready for self-government; to put it bluntly, that we are not capable of it. In fact, you know, I suspect that misgivings of this kind are behind some of the hesitations over independence.

PHS   Of course, much unionist propaganda undermines Scottish self-confidence, presumably with the intention of leading to this sort of conclusion. Not only the Conservatives are guilty of this. As Colin Kirkwood said in a recent book: 'Labourism has played on our insecurity and our fear of freedom, by denouncing Scottish nationalism as separatist.'[25] The Liberal Democrats do the same. A good deal of Scottish education, with its Anglocentric bias, tends to have the same result.

   In fact, Scotland is obviously far more highly prepared for self-government than the great majority of countries who have achieved it and carried it through with success. We have the traditions and still some of the institutions of centuries of independence, when we made a distinguished contribution to European civilisation, in spite of constant attack and invasion by a more powerful neighbour. The civil service and the administrative machine is already in place.

Scots have played a major role in the development of other countries in Europe, and, in more recent times, in the Commonwealth. At Westminster many of the leading figures in all parties are Scottish. There is no doubt that we have plenty of men and women of ability, so many that we constantly export them.

Is it argued that we are torn by disagreement and an incapacity to co-operate? I doubt if this is truer of Scotland than it is of England. In both countries it is probably the result of the Westminster style of confrontational politics, encouraged by the old two party, first-past-the-post system and even by the design of the House. In Scotland there is a wide measure of consensus on what needs to be done. Once we have settled the constitutional issue, I think that this consensus would prevail in the Scottish parliament. But let us keep this whole thing in proportion. We have no disagreements in Scotland so strong that we are tempted to settle them by violence. In this, as in many other aspects, we are in a very fortunate position.

SF To end this part of our discussion on a practical point, what would be the effect of independence on pensions and social security payments?

PHS Private pensions would continue as before. Responsibility for state pensions and social security benefits would be transferred to the Scottish government, after a negotiated transfer of the records and a share of the accumulated deposits. At present state pensions and benefits in the UK are below the European average. The UK government has refused to accept the Social Chapter which is intended to ensure fair and equal social conditions in all the member states. A Scottish government, with our traditions in these matters, would certainly want to raise social provision at least to the general European standard. At present they are well below. Scotland has a GDP her head of £8,805 which is a third higher than Ireland where it is £6,761; but the single old age pension in Ireland is £62.43 compared to the British rate of £54.15. In Luxemburg it is about £100.

SF Talking about government offices of this kind reminds me that there are some offices in Scotland which do not work for the whole of the UK. Independence would presumably mean a loss of jobs in cases like that.

PHS There are far more functions in Scotland carried out from offices in England and Wales than the other way round. Where do you have to apply for your driving or TV licence and who handles your income tax? I have noticed in recent years that functions of all kinds are increasingly 'rationalised' to the south. Independence would certainly repatriate many of these lost jobs. But that will be only a small part of the new opportunities and employment that will come with independence. Decision-making in Scotland would mean a marked increase in satisfying and well-paid jobs. Independence would mean a surge of activity to revitalise Scotland and deal with the consequences of past neglect.

One of the most depressing symptoms of that neglect and misgovernment has been the steady loss of population through emigration because of the lack of employment at home. There was a loss of 156,000 in the 1980s and the Register General predicts a further loss of 130,000 in the 90s. In most countries in the world population is increasing, including England, Wales and Northern Ireland; Scotland is a conspicuous exception. Successive British governments have ignored this problem. To them it seems peripheral and unimportant, like other matters of purely Scottish concern. A Scottish government would have a very different attitude.

4. THE EUROPEAN DIMENSION

SF   Many of the points you have been making are based
on the assumption that an independent Scotland would be
a member of the European Community. Can we be sure of
that? A whole succession of Conservative ministers have
argued that Scotland (but not England, apparently) would
have to re-apply for membership and that this would be a
long and difficult process. Ian Lang, for instance, said in a
speech on 8 July 1991: 'If Scotland were to leave the UK,
as the SNP propose, it would find itself at the back of an
ever-lengthening queue to get back in'.[26]

PHS   This sort of thing is typical, I am sorry to say, of the
trumped-up arguments used by the Unionists to try to
deflect and undermine Scottish aspirations. They seem to
be prepared to say anything without regard for truth, logic
or consistency, as long as it suits their case. It is bad enough
to find English ministers doing it, but it is particularly
repulsive when Scots run down their own country. The
speech of Ian Lang which you mention is even more
abhorrent because he made it in Strasburg. He seems to
have been trying to provoke other European governments
into an attitude harmful to Scotland.
    The fact is that the UK was created by the Treaty of
Union between Scotland and England in 1707. If one party
decides to withdraw from the Treaty, then Scotland and
England revert to their previous status as independent
countries. Under international law they would both inherit
the other treaty rights and obligations of the former United
Kingdom and that includes membership of the European

Community. There is no provision in the Treaty of Rome for the withdrawal or expulsion of a member state, or part of one, from the Community. This applies to both Scotland and England in precisely the same way. It is arrogant nonsense to pretend that England has some special privilege in the matter. We should both have to negotiate some consequential adjustments to such matters as voting weight in the Council, membership of the Parliament and of the Commission. Since there is no need for a new application, no protracted negotiation and no risk of opposition or veto would arise.

The European authorities who are best qualified to judge are in agreement about this. At the risk of some repetition, let me quote one or two of them.

Emile Noël, former Secretary General of the European Commission:

> There is no precedent and no provision for the expulsion of a member state, therefore Scottish independence would create two new member states out of one. They would have equal status with each other and the other 11 states. The remainder of the United Kingdom would not be in a more powerful position than Scotland ... Anyone who is attacking the claim in respect of one country is attacking it in respect of the other. It is not possible to divide the cases.[27]

Lord Mackenzie-Stuart, a former judge and President of the European Court of Justice:

> Independence would leave Scotland and 'something called the rest' in the same legal boat. If Scotland had to re-apply, so would the rest ... I am puzzled at the suggestion that there would be a difference in the status of Scotland and the rest of the United Kingdom in terms of Community law if the Act of Union was dissolved.[28]

Eamonn Gallagher, a former Director General of the European Commission and recently EC ambassador to the

United Nations:

> In my view, there could be no sustainable legal or political objection to separate Scottish membership of the European Community.[29]

We should remember, too, the importance to Europe of Scottish stocks of oil and fish. At a time when the Community is like to expand by the admission of many new members, there could be no tenable objection to Scotland's continued membership.

SF It has been suggested by Douglas Hurd[30] and other Conservative ministers that countries with independence movements of their own, such as Spain, would oppose or even veto Scottish membership.

PHS The possibility of veto would only arise if Scotland had to apply for admission. This would then require the unanimous agreement of the existing members. Since Scotland is already within the Community, the veto would work the other way. In the highly improbable supposition that another member might propose the expulsion of Scotland (although as I have said, there is no precedent of Treaty provision for such a move), then this would require the unanimous agreement of all the member states, and any one member could veto it. This is the realm of fantasy. There is not the slightest evidence that any member state would oppose the membership of such a valuable partner as Scotland, but many assurances to the contrary, including one, for example, from the Spanish Foreign Ministry. We have, after all, centuries of experience of fruitful co-operation with the rest of Europe. If any country has a history of awkward insularity which still continues to cause difficulty, it is England.

SF The same Conservative Ministers have repeatedly told us that Scotland as an independent member would be one of the smaller members with only a very small voice in the affairs of the Community. To quote Hurd again: 'The United Kingdom has far more clout in guiding the direction of the Community and in defending the interests of our people than smaller states can have'.[31] Are we in a better position as part of the UK than we would be on our own?

PHS Better a small voice than no voice at all. The UK delegation is the voice of the UK government. For more than a decade it has been formed by a party which has been rejected by the Scottish electorate. It follows an ideology and carries out policies of which we disapprove. Whenever the views of the interests of Scotland and England differ, as they frequently do, a government of the UK must give preference, for good democratic reasons, to those of England. We are different in climate, geology, systems of law and education, industrial structure, the nature of our farming, the relative importance of fishing. For most of the time, therefore, Scotland under the present arrangements is either misrepresented or not represented at all.

The use of the word 'clout' by Douglas Hurd, and quite often by his Conservative colleagues is a give-away. It shows, I think, that they cling to the notion that Britain is still a great power with a special mission in the world. It is part of the explanation of their attitude to Scotland.

But it is true, in any case, that the smaller member states are of as little account as Hurd would have us believe? John Major has been strenuously advocating the widening of the European Community by the admission of many new members. (Scotland, in his view, remains of course an exception.) Many of these potential new members are of a comparable size to Scotland. Do Hurd and Major tell them that they will be of insignificant importance within the Community?

The fact is that international organisations are of more benefit to small countries than to larger ones. The tendency of these organisations is to curb the ability of larger countries to bully the smaller. They have something of the ethos of clubs in which all members have equal privileges and an equal right to be heard. In the United Nations all members, no matter how large or small, have the same single vote. This is true also in the European Community as far as decisions on new policies are concerned. These require unanimity and therefore every member has the right to veto, which is why the Danish referendum on the Maastricht Treaty was of such consequence. But what, you will ask, about the system of weighted voting?

This is the system which applies to the implementation of new policies and therefore to most routine business. It takes account of the differences in the size of population of the member states. France, Germany, Italy, and the UK each have 10 votes. Spain has 8. Belgium, Greece, the Netherlands and Portugal have 5, Denmark and Ireland 3 and Luxemburg 2. A majority requires 54 votes out of a total of 76. Even if the four larger countries vote together, therefore, they cannot achieve a majority without the support of at least two of the smaller ones. The system is deliberately designed to prevent the larger countries imposing their will on the rest. Douglas Hurd is simply misrepresenting the position when he tries to persuade us that the UK with 10 votes is all powerful and that an independent Scotland with 3 would have no influence on decisions.

SF What will be the effect of the enlargement of the Community by the admission of many new members, Norway, Sweden, Finland, Austria, Switzerland and the countries of eastern Europe?

PHS I think that this will be a very healthy development. It will extend co-operation, and freedom of movement and trade, over a wider area, which will be almost the whole of Europe and not merely part of it. It will give expression to the diversity of Europe which is one of its valuable qualities. It will greatly increase the number of smaller countries within the membership and therefore make it even more necessary than it is already for the Community to respect their views and safeguard their interests. This is a Europe where an independent Scotland would be very much at home and could make a useful contribution. The smaller countries together would reduce the risk of the domination of Europe by one or two of the larger member states. Scottish membership of the Community would be of benefit, not only to Scotland, but to Europe as a whole.

SF But it will be difficult, or impossible, to continue the existing procedures of the Community with such an enlarged membership. This might well lead to a reduction in the privileges of the smaller countries. I hear that there are already suggestions that they should lose their right to appoint a commissioner and succeed by rotation to the presidency.

PHS I agree that some changes will have to be made. But remember that they will require the unanimous consent of all the smaller member states and are therefore unlikely to be greatly to their detriment. Of course, the sooner Scotland becomes a member in our own right the better, so that we can play a part in this evolution.

SF You do not see any inconsistency in simultaneously advocating Scottish independence and proposing to surrender a considerable degree of Scottish sovereignty to the Community?

PHS No. We should acquire the same degree of independence and sovereignty as any other member state of the Community. That is infinitely more than our present invisibility and impotence. Membership of the Community certainly involves the pooling of sovereignty, but the member states have accepted this deliberately and voluntarily because of the advantages which it brings. The smaller countries, in particular, have found that it gives them greater prosperity and self-confidence because their views and national interests can no longer be ignored by their larger neighbours.

The former Prime Minister of Ireland, Garret FitzGerald, addressed precisely this question in an article in the *Irish Times*:

> If we had not been independent during the first half of this century, and if we had joined the Community as part of a recalcitrant and unenthusiastic United Kingdom, we would have had neither the capacity to secure our interests within the Community nor an opportunity to express our personality and make our own distinctive, if necessarily modest, contribution to the development of this new political structure for Europe.[32]

FitzGerald's conclusion was that Irish membership of the Community was the 'ultimate justification' of the movement for national independence. Leaders of other small member states have said much the same. They have found that membership of the Community has given them greater security for their national identity and more influence on events than they would have outside it.

Mary Robinson, the President of Ireland, spoke similarly when she was on a visit to Scotland in June 1992: 'There has been a great sense of liberation. We have become more sure of our own Irish identity in the context of being equal partners in Europe. It meant we no longer simply define ourselves in terms of our relationship with Britain. We are Irish but we are also European.' And she added: 'Ireland and Scotland have so much in common yet there are very few institutional links that recognise this. We must build them up.'[33] This is absolutely right. An independent

Scotland within the European Community would have a great deal in common with Ireland and with the Scandinavian countries which are likely to join the Community soon. Together on matters of common interest we should have a voting strength of up to 18.

In a Europe where virtually every country has joined, or is seeking to join, the Community, an independent Scotland which stood outside would be in splendid, but unrewarding, isolation.

SF Could I repeat a question which Allan Massie addressed to you in an article in the *Scotsman*: 'If the United Kingdom, joined by language, history, old friendships, consanguinity, a degree of common culture can't hold together as a political structure, why should we suppose that Europe, divided in all these respects, has much chance of doing so?'[34]

PHS In fact, we do not have a great deal in common in history, culture and so forth with the rest of Europe. We were allied with France and closely associated with many other countries in Europe for centuries. The Union of 1707 and the new European union which is now emerging are quite different in character. In 1707 we were forced to accept disguised annexation by the manipulation and bribery of a small ruling class and by the implied threat of invasion and the imposition of worse terms. The Treaty of Union deprived us of our parliament and our international identity and there was no machinery to prevent violations of the Treaty or provide for its amendment. The European Community is a voluntary association of states for their mutual benefit. They retain their international identities and their parliaments. There are international courts to prevent violations and arrangements for amendment by agreement.

The Treaty of Union was like conscription into the navy by press gang, where your protests are ignored and where you have to do what you are told and make the best of it. The European Community is a club where Scotland could recover the status, rights and privileges which we lost in 1707.

SF   What about regionalism? I have seen claims by Labour and Liberal Democrat spokesmen that Scotland's aspirations could be met by an increased emphasis on regionalism in Europe and that the nation states will gradually fade away in favour of a Europe of the regions.

PHS   This is so far from reality that it must be a deliberate attempt to mislead. The transfer of real power to the regions (and Scotland is not a region in any case) is simply not on the European agenda. Scotland can only play its proper and due part in Europe when it becomes a member state like any other.

5. DEVOLUTION:
A USEFUL FIRST STEP?

SF Many people, including apparently most of the Scottish electorate, think that a cautious step-by-step approach might be the best way forward. In other words, should we try the half-way house of devolution before going the whole way to independence? I know, of course, that Labour and the Liberal Democrats advocate devolution not as a step towards independence but as an end in itself. Indeed, they argue that it is the best way to prevent independence and, as they say, the 'break-up of the United Kingdom'. Even so, it might the quickest and easiest way to make progress. We could feel our way forward with a parliament with limited powers before deciding if we want to accept full responsibility, the 'L-plate' approach. It might even turn out to be enough by itself.

PHS It is unlikely to be easier and quicker. We can decide on independence for ourselves by demonstrating through an election or referendum that that is what a majority of us want. Devolution has to be conceded by the UK parliament and that will only happen if you have a UK government committed to the idea and determined to carry it through. Experience suggests that this is improbable. Since 1889 no fewer than 34 Scottish Home Rule Bills have been presented to the House of Commons. All have been lapsed in spite of the support, in nearly every case, of a majority of the Scottish MPs.

English voters seem to be quite happy with a permanent Conservative one-party state. Even if there were another Labour government, or a Labour/Liberal Democrat coalition, the Scottish constitutional question might not be high among their priorities. We have had both Labour and Liberal Democrat governments in the past who were, in theory, committed to Scottish Home Rule, but failed to enact it. If these parties were to introduce a Bill, every UK Department of State would be careful at the drafting state to see that it lost as little of its own power and influence as possible. During the debates in Parliament, the Bill would be at the mercy of the whims and bright ideas which happened to catch the fancy of the overwhelming English majority in both Houses. That is what happened last time when we had the 40% rule and all the rest of it.

SF Yes, I see that; but even if independence won a clear majority in a referendum, or the SNP most of the seats in an election, you would still have to have negotiations.

PHS Certainly, but the principle would have been established and the negotiations would be on the consequential arrangements, division of assets and the like. Some 50 member states of the Commonwealth, all now happily independent, have gone through this process. It is well understood; there are plenty of precedents and it has never caused any particular difficulty.

SF Let us for the moment assume that a Devolution Bill had survived all the parliamentary hurdles, and that you had a devolved parliament in Edinburgh. Would that not be a considerable improvement on the present state of affairs?

PHS I think so, because you would have an elected body which could form a view on the problems and opportunities which face us and legislate to deal with some of them. It would be a step in the right direction, but so timid and half-hearted a step that it would do more to arouse expectations than to satisfy them.

SF Would it not give us many of the benefits that you expect from independence?

PHS Not in the least and for three main reasons. In the first place, it would be confusing and unstable. Ultimate power and most of the most important decisions would still remain in London. There would be an inevitable tendency towards tension and disagreement over both policy and financial allocations to Scotland, especially when different parties were in power in Edinburgh and London. There is also the notorious West Lothian question,[35] even if its significance has been greatly exaggerated. Second, we would still not be able to decide for ourselves many matters of the greatest possible concern to us. This includes major economic policy as well as such questions as whether we should have nuclear reprocessing at Dounreay and nuclear submarines on the Clyde. Thirdly, we should still have no international identity and no membership in our own right of international organisations, including the European Community. The difference between independence and devolution is more than one of degree. There is all the difference in the world between a country free to take its own decisions and participate fully in international relations, and a province, even if it has some degree of internal self-government.

For all these reasons, devolution would be unlikely to bring the sense of liberation and opportunity and the stimulation of achievement and progress which independence has brought to so many countries. Have you ever heard of a country which celebrates Devolution Day?

SF But there are proposals in the European Community to pay more attention to the regions and give them a bigger say.

PHS There has been a great deal of talk about this, but no essential change in the way decisions are made in the Community. The Treaty of Maastricht proposes to set up a Committee of the Regions, but its only function would be to express opinions. The member states will remain, in Douglas Hurd's phrase, the building blocks of the Community. Their views and interests have to be taken into account and they make the decisions. Scotland has at least as much right as any other historic nation of Europe to this status and should not settle for anything less.

In any case, Scotland at present does not qualify as a region in the sense in which the word is understood in Europe. Regions in Europe, such as the German Länder, have their own parliaments or assemblies. Scotland does not.

SF Does the European Parliament offer Scotland a forum in which we can make our views known?

PHS Winnie Ewing, so far the only SNP member, has certainly used it for this purpose to very good effect. The powers of the European Parliament are very limited, but they will increase and Maastricht is a step in this direction. The allocation of seats in the parliament is an example of the advantages which follow from independence and membership. Scotland as part of the UK has 8 seats. Denmark, with about the same population as Scotland, has 16.

SF The Liberal Democrats, and to some extent Labour and even some prominent Conservatives, have proposed to meet some of the difficulties of devolution by proposing federalism through the UK. Would that be of any benefit to Scotland?

PHS The only difficulty it solves is the West Lothian question which, if it is a problem at all, is one for the Westminster parliament, not for Scotland. It would give neither increased power nor international identity to Scotland. On the contrary, it would involve the risk of a drastic deterioration of the already diminished status of Scotland.

Usually the federalists propose the division of England into a number of regions, each with its own assembly or sub-parliament. In such an arrangement, Scotland would inevitably sink into the status of just another English region. One Labour MP, Tony Worthington, has recognised this and proposed that England, Wales, Northern Ireland and Scotland should each have their own parliaments, as well as a common British one.[36] This is more logical, but why have a British parliament at all, when most of the subjects of common interest are likely to be settled by the Community? Even Worthington himself admits that his idea will be difficult to sell to the English who think that they have an English parliament already and who have never shown much enthusiasm for any kind of federalism.

In fact all talk about federalism is academic because it is not something which we can decide for ourselves. It can only happen if the English electorate are converted to the idea and of that there is no sign.

SF When you speak of logic, I am reminded that the former Conservative cabinet minister, John Biffen, said recently that independence was more logical than devolution, and that if he were Scottish he would want full membership of the European Community and not to be a Euro-region.[37]

PHS He is right on both points. Of course, he is not the only prominent Conservative to say that he would prefer independence to devolution. There is a contradiction among Conservatives about this. One of the favourite arguments of many of them against devolution is that it would lead inevitably to independence, and in this case they imply that this would be worse and not better. They are pulling in opposite directions.

SF Devolution offers much less to Scotland than independence; it is not necessarily easier to achieve and federalism is more of a complication than an advantage. Why then do Labour and the Liberal Democrats argue for a Scottish parliament, but insist that it should go no further than devolution within the UK, with most of the important functions remaining at Westminster?

PHS   This puzzles me. The arguments which lead them to see the urgent need for a Scottish parliament should lead them logically, as some prominent Liberals have admitted, to the conclusion that the best policy for Scotland is independence with our own membership of the European Community. Most of their leaders tell us endlessly that the Union of 1707 must be preserved at all costs, although they produce no satisfactory explanation of this position, which is more an act of faith than a reasonable policy. They do not seem to grasp the radical change introduced by membership of the European Community. It has removed all the old objections to independence. Westminster is now very clearly a superfluous and harmful level of government as far as Scotland is concerned.

Labour and the Liberal Democrats are, in any case, trapped in a contradiction. The Constitutional Convention, which they established, was based on the report, *A Claim of Right for Scotland*, drawn, up by the Constitutional Steering Committee in 1988.[38] This report was a very thorough and frank analysis of the way in which the Union of 1707 has worked to the disadvantage of Scotland. It concluded that the Union had 'failed Scotland'; that 'the Union has always been, and remains, a threat to the survival of a distinctive culture in Scotland'; that 'the United Kingdom has been an anomaly from its inception and is a glaring anomaly now'. How is it possible for these same parties to argue now that the Union should be preserved?

So why does the leadership of Labour and the Liberal Democrats stick at the thoroughly unsatisfactory half-way house of devolution? Of course, we are all brought up under great pressure to believe that Britain or the UK is part of the natural order of things. It takes a certain amount of intellectual courage to think beyond that. Then there are certain attitudes which affect long-standing members of the Labour Party as a consequence of vague ideas of socialist internationalism. Although they deplore imperialism elsewhere, they have an illogical feeling that concern for Britain is more international and enlightened than concern for Scotland. This is particularly ironic when you consider how internationally minded Scotland has always been; but our educational system generally results in a profound ignorance of our own history.

Of course, Labour and the Liberal Democrats are British parties and it is therefore natural for them to think in British terms. A strong motive for both of them to hold on to the Union is that they want their Scottish seats to give them a better chance of power, or a share of power, at Westminster. Many of their MPs have ambitions for British, and not, Scottish, office. John Smith, for instance, could not be leader of the British Labour Party with a Scottish constituency if Scotland was independent.

Given all the pressures, it is not surprising that some people should think predominantly in British terms; but it is unfortunate and short-sighted. An independent, and therefore more contented and prosperous, Scotland is in the interest of England and our other partners in Europe as well as our own. An independent Scotland will make a better neighbour and trading partner than a Scotland ignored, frustrated and impeded.

6. NATIONALISM, THE ARMY AND THE MONARCHY

SF The party which stands for Scottish Independence within the European Community is the Scottish National Party. Its supporters are usually called nationalists and its philosophy nationalism. To many people these words are negative, pejorative, even frightening. Might this not be an obstacle to the cause of Scottish independence?

PHS Yes, I agree that this is quite possible. Like many other words used in political discussion, nationalism can be used in different senses, some of which are in flat contradiction to others. On the whole, the word has a bad press. You quite often hear, for instance, the television news blaming 'the destructive force of nationalism' for some violent outrage or other. To blame nationalism for its excesses is like condemning all religion for the Inquisition or sectarian killing in Belfast. In fact, the parallel is quite close. Religion can mean compassion, morality and kindness, but also intolerance and oppression. Similarly, a desire of one country to impose its will on others can be called nationalism; but so can the resistance to the military attack and occupation and the liberation from it.

It would be less confusing if we could all agree to call the oppressors the imperialists and the liberators nationalists; but the confusion is thoroughly established. Peter Alter, who wrote a recent book on the subject, says that the word can be used both for oppression and for 'forces striving for political, social, economic and cultural emancipation.'[39] The confusion is even worse in some other countries, especially Germany, where some of the worst political elements, such as the Nazis, have been called nationalist. But, of course, like the Conservative Party, they can also be called right-wing. Nationalism is not the only word subject to this sort of confusion.

But there is doubt at all where Scottish nationalism stands. It is not, and never has been at any time in history, aggressive, but wants only good relations and co-operation with other countries. It is entirely on the side of democracy and emancipation.

SF   But there have been attempts by political opponents to represent it as something quite different.

PHS   Certainly. There were some particularly unscrupulous examples during the last General Election. Michael Heseltine in a speech in Edinburgh on 7 April said that nationalism 'had brought extremism in France, fascism in Germany, and eastern Europe convulsed by ethnic hatred and racial bitterness ... It is about the young people sent to tear each other apart. That's what nationalism has always been about'.[40] As a statement on its own, using the word, nationalism, in its most negative sense, that is fair enough; but in the context of his speech it was clear that Heseltine was trying to blacken the SNP with the same brush.

For the Labour Party, Brian Wilson and Jean McFadden also indulged in the same kind of outrageous distortion. Wilson implied in an article in *New Statesman and Society*[41] that there was affinity between the SNP and the Nazis on the flimsy grounds that they were both known by initials and had a 'funny symbol', and Jean McFadden made much the same point in the *Herald*.[42]

SF   But what about the horrifying events which are going on in what used to be Yugoslavia? Are they not the result of nationalism?

PHS Of a kind, but it is something quite different from what we are discussing in Scotland. The Balkans are notorious for deep-rooted enmities which were submerged under Tito and are now all the stronger in consequence. The situation is worse because the largest of the countries, Serbia, is aggressive and expansionist. There is simply no parallel with our situation. Scottish nationalism is liberal and civic, not ethnic nor intolerant. The SNP would welcome everyone living in Scotland to Scottish citizenship, if they want it. Many residents of English or other origin are supporters of the SNP because they see the need for independence.

It is the nationalism of the big countries which can be chauvinistic, aggressive and intolerant. As Joyce McMillan wrote recently, of Britain and France in particular, 'their consciousness is centralising in tendency, and uncomfortable with cultural difference. It is characterised above all by the assumption that its own culture is a norm and a good to which all others should aspire.'[43] Small nations understand that they are just one culture among many, and they are ready to welcome for others the same freedom which they value for themselves. They have no ambition to impose their will on anyone else. They are always on the side of peace. That is why the future of civilised values is safer in the hands of small nations and why their emancipation is desirable, not only for their own sake, but for the benefit of the rest of the world as well.

SF How then would you define nationalism and the Scottish variety in particular?

PHS I should say that it was an affection for one's native place, a sense of identification with one's fellow citizens, past, present and future and a desire to make a contribution to our common welfare. Robert Burns said that he wanted to make a song for Scotland's sake. That is an example of this impulse. It includes, too, respect for the nationality of others and a wish to co-operate with them. It does not mean, in the Scottish case at least, any sense of superiority and a wish to lord it over others. We do not feel better than other people, but we do feel that our distinctive attitudes and qualities are a valuable contribution to human diversity and that we have the same right as other nations to run our own affairs.

SF Do you not detect in Scotland some resentment, hostility or dislike towards the English?

PHS Considering our historical experience and the current disregard of Scottish views and aspirations, that is to be expected. As I have said before, one of the benefits of independence is that it will remove the causes of these negative feelings and give an opportunity for genuine co-operation and much better relations with England.

SF You say that Scotland has never been aggressive, but many people regard the Scottish military tradition as an essential part of the Scottish identity. There is nothing very pacific about that.

PHS Allan Massie, to give an example of this, wrote in an article in the *Scotsman*: 'Let those pretend that there has been no loyalty to the idea of Britain ... consider the battle honours of the Scottish regiments, all won in wars which were British, neither English nor Scots.'[44] I do not think that anyone denies that Scots have felt loyalty to Britain and that millions of them have died in the cause; but is that something in which we should take unqualified pride and satisfaction? This is an aspect of Britain's imperial past which is now well behind us. Even so, I think that it is very doubtful that the Scots who took part thought of themselves as wholly, or predominantly, British. Helen Bannerman spent years in India as the wife of a Scottish officer in the Victorian heyday of the British Raj. From their letters, it is clear that they thought of themselves as Scots, and of Scotland first and the Empire second.[45] This was probably typical and I have little doubt that Scots in the British army to this day have the same sense of priorities.

Of course, there was much that was admirable in the courage and endurance of the soldier; but there must also be shame in the way in which the British state exploited these qualities, and Scottish sentiment, for its own purposes. There is no more cynical example of this than the raising of the Highland regiments in the 18th century. The kilt and the pipes were prohibited in Scotland, but used in the army as an inducement to recruitment. It was General Wolfe, the hero of Quebec, who was considered to be unusually civilised and humane among army officers of his time, who proposed to raise Highland companies. He advocated it in a letter in which he said: 'They are hardy, intrepid, accustomed to a rough country, and no great mischief if they fall. How can you better employ a secret enemy than by making his end conducive to the common good?'[46]

One can understand why Tom Nairn wrote recently: 'It is precisely because popular Scottish militarism has become so identified with Union, Empire and extra-national causes, that the sooner we are rid of it the better.'[47]

SF What about the defence of an independent Scotland?

PHS If we had kept our independence we should have been involved in many fewer wars in the last 300 years, but that does not affect the present. We are now in a very new situation. The perceived external threat to western Europe has vanished with the end of the Soviet Union. European defence policy has still to adjust to the new situation, but Europe is already so integrated that some common arrangement must follow. An independent Scotland would be at least as capable as any other member state of comparable size of maintaining the forces needed for a contribution to this common defence and to any peace-keeping operations in other parts of the world in which we may decide to take part. The Scottish regiments would adapt admirably to this role. Like most of the rest of Europe we should, of course, have no nuclear weapons and that would make us more secure and not less.

SF   Shall we lose jobs in the defence industries?

PHS   Defence industries everywhere must lose jobs because, fortunately, the military threat is less. This is a positive development because the fewer arms that are manufactured and traded the better. Everything possible should be done to provide alternative jobs, but it would be unacceptable to continue to produce unnecessary and dangerous weapons simply to provide employment. Some manufacture will still be needed. At present, as George Rosie has shown, Scotland does not get a fair share of UK defence procurement.[48] An independent Scotland in the single European market would be able to compete on more equal terms.

SF   To turn to a different, but perhaps related point, is the monarchy an obstacle to Scottish independence?

PHS   The monarchy is often thought to be a symbol of Britishness, and it is openly used to promote the British state. It is also a symbol of the Commonwealth, an association of independent countries which have exercised their right of self-determination. Scotland will be in precisely the same position and the monarchy will be no more of an obstacle to Scottish independence than it was for Canada, New Zealand and all the others. After independence it will be for the Scottish people to decide whether they wish to regard the Queen as Head of State. If they do, she would then be Queen of Scotland as she is Queen of Canada and of other countries in the Commonwealth. Her role would, of course, as elsewhere, be purely ceremonial and symbolic.

Nor will independence necessarily mean the end of a feeling of Britishness. The Scottish identity has been weakened by the Union, but it has not been destroyed by it. Similarly, whatever is constructive about a feeling of Britishness can continue after independence. The obvious parallel is with Norway which is now more at ease with the idea of Scandinavia than it was before the achievement of independence. An independent Scotland will have no difficulty in accommodating a feeling of shared experience with the other nations of the British Isles, with the other small nations of northern Europe and with Europe as a whole. People like Allan Massie, who have a sentimental attachment to Britishness, should welcome the healthier and more equal relationship which will come with independence.

7. SCOTTISH INDEPENDENCE — WHY NOT?

SF We have discussed the reasons which might explain why the leadership of Labour and the Liberal Democrats want to go no further than devolution. Why do you suppose it is that the Conservatives and those who vote for them want to preserve the constitutional status quo? After all it is very unusual, perhaps unique, for a substantial group of people in a country to resist, and actively campaign against the freedom to run their own affairs.

PHS I agree that this is an extraordinary state of affairs which we should discuss. It is true that the Conservatives took this position under Margaret Thatcher and continued it with even more frenzy under John Major, but it has not always been their policy. You remember that Edward Heath in his Declaration of Perth of 1968 promised a Scottish assembly with control over Scottish affairs. This was endorsed by the Scottish Conference of the Conservative Party by a large majority. At the time of the referendum in 1979, when Thatcher was already leader, their official line was to vote 'no' in order to get a stronger Scottish assembly with powers of taxation and proportional representation, two points which they then described as essential, although they later used them as objections to the Constitutional Convention proposals. They also promised the immediate calling of a constitutional conference to improve the government of Scotland, but forgot about this as soon as the promise had served its purpose.

The fact is that the Conservative Party is not like other parties where the views of the members largely determine policy and where this imposes a certain consistency. With the Conservatives the leader decides and can usually rely on party loyalty to get his or her own way. So under Heath, they are for constitutional change; under Thatcher and Major, they are against it. It is the English leadership which decides the policy, not the members in Scotland. It is even more mysterious when we know from opinion polls that a considerable proportion of their supporters are in favour of devolution or independence.

SF Of course many people vote Conservative for reasons other than the constitutional issue.

PHS Certainly. There are all sorts of reasons, habits, instincts and prejudices, many of them quite irrational. There is traditional Conservatism which is content with the way things are and distrusts change, even if the Conservatives have in fact been changing things at a furious pace in the last thirteen years. Some older people, those who are comfortable financially and those who do not think much about politics at all, are often in this category. They are part of the 'culture of contentment', which J.K. Galbraith says has turned the comfortable masses in the western world against any challenge to the *status quo*.[49] Then there are the business Conservatives, such as the tycoons who finance the Party, who assume, rightly or wrongly, that the Conservatives exist to promote their interest. They are afraid of uncertainty and change, and of the possibility of a government that would harm their business, although a Scottish government would have every incentive to promote a healthy economy.

SF You are suggesting, I think, that these categories of people, who exist in every country, will always vote Conservative, irrespective of the position which the Party might be taking at the time on the constitutional question. If that is so, they cannot have any strong feelings about the constitution or attach much importance to it.

PHS Presumably that is so, but we have to remember that many people read only London newspapers, perhaps even the bigoted Tory tabloids, and watch mainly London-based television broadcasts. They may have heard very little about the case for independence or the benefits which it would bring both to the country and to them personally.

SF Yes, but there are clearly people who heard some of the arguments but are positively and strongly opposed to any form of Scottish parliament and particularly to independence.

PHS Again there are many reasons and some of them unconscious and irrational. The British state and all its agencies has centuries of acquired skill in propaganda, persuasion and manipulation. I have made a study over many years of the way in which the Union came about in 1707, and I must admit that even then the skill of the English officials in these matters was impressive. Our schools, consciously or unconsciously, have assisted the process; they have left most of us with a very distorted view of Scottish history and achievement. Our culture has been denigrated and our self-confidence undermined. In these circumstances, it is not in the least surprising that many Scots have accepted the myth of English superiority, the virtues of the Mother of Parliaments and all the rest of it. It follows that they should feel we are lucky to be associated with them and that we should cling to the association.

SF Does that mean that many people in Scotland are suffering from a massive inferiority complex and feelings of insecurity and that this determines the way they respond to the constitutional issue?

PHS Yes. I think it explains why it was possible for the Unionists in all the UK parties at the time of the referendum and in the election of 1992 to play on these fears and insecurity without having to address the rational argument. But we should not be too pessimistic about this. Given all the years of brainwashing, all the power of the state, and all the millions of pounds spent on propaganda, it is remarkable how many people stood up against the barrage and saw through it. In spite of all the pressures, our national self-confidence is increasing and cannot be denied much longer.

SF So far, we have been talking about the motives of the manipulated. What about those of the manipulators? Why is the leadership of the Conservative Party in Scotland and England now so opposed to constitutional change?

PHS You are right, in this connection at least, to distinguish between the Conservative Party in Scotland and in England because different considerations apply. For the Conservatives in Scotland, the Union gives them a chance to hold on to power, and all the jobs, appointments and honours that go with it, on the back of the English vote. They have been doing this for thirteen years. Any Scottish MP who was employable at all could be confident of a ministerial appointment. They shamelessly packed all the boards and quangos that lie within the vast patronage of the Secretary of State with their supporters and fellow travellers. They have forced on us their ideological whims and excesses by imposing policies which had been clearly rejected by the Scottish people. This whole period of Conservative rule has been a monstrous abuse of power by men who had no democratic right to it. It has been shameful; but you can see why they want to hold on to it and why they are such uncritical enthusiasts for the Union.

The Conservatives seem to assume that they would have no chance of power, or a share of it, in an independent

Scotland. They are wrong about this. As I have said, an independent Scotland would certainly have proportional representation. No party would have a share of seats grossly in excess of their share of the vote, as Labour has under the present system. A genuinely Scottish Conservative Party, which opted for independence and the Scottish interest, would probably have a strong voice in the Scottish parliament.

The present attitude of the Conservative Party deprives them of the votes of many people who would be among the natural supporters of a Conservative Party which defended, instead of resisting, Scottish aspirations. Michael Fry, who is a prominent, if unorthodox, Conservative, is disturbed by this:

> Scottish Conservatives have got themselves into an extraordinary position where national sentiment actually works against us, something which would be inconceivable for any other Conservative party in any other land. Alone among the Conservative parties of the world, the Scottish one tells its country that nationhood counts for nothing. Can we still then define ourselves as a Conservative party? Is not an unpatriotic Conservative party a meaningless abstraction?[50]

SF The attitude of present-day Scottish Conservative politicians is very similar to that of the lords in the Scottish parliament of 1707 who supported the Union because it suited their own private interest and because they were well rewarded by the English government. This applies, as it always does, only to those on the gravy train and not to those who are merely persuaded to vote for them and get nothing for it at all. But what about the Conservative Party machine in England? If they really believe, as they often claim, that Scotland is a financial liability, then Scottish independence should suit them. Politically it would make their hold on power in England even more certain, because Scotland

tends to give more members to the opposition benches than
to the Conservative ones. In opposing Scottish independence they seem to be harming their own interests. What are
their motives?

PHS   Their attitude is so irrational and their explanations
so unconvincing that this is all very mysterious. As usual,
most of them are presumably simply following the leader, so
it is John Major that we have to try to understand. Of course
it is quite possible, since Conservatives seem only to meet
and listen to Conservatives, that he has simply taken the
advice of his Scottish ministers and it is not difficult to guess
what that would be. For a clue we should look at his own
speeches, always on the understanding that he may not
want to admit his real motives.

Major's Scottish policy is inconsistent, illogical and
marked by a bias against Scotland which he does not show
against any other country. He is in favour of self-determination for the Falkland Islands, Latvia, Lithuania, Estonia
and almost any other country you can think of, but not for
Scotland. He is anxious to give a parliament to Northern
Ireland, which has shown no great desire for it, but refuses
it to Scotland, where the last four General Elections and
every opinion poll since polls began have shown an overwhelming majority in favour of it. He admits that Scotland
is an ancient and proud nation. In the European context he
defends the right of nations to make their own decisions and
resist excessive centralisation in Brussels. But this insist-
ence on susidiarity does not apply to Scotland. Within the
UK he insists on the centralising right of Westminster to
impose its will on Scotland. Major is in favour of the
widening of the European Community by the admission of
many new members, but again he is utterly opposed to
Scottish membership. Why must we always be the exception? Is there some powerful motive which makes Major
deny to Scotland the rights of self-determination, democ-

racy, national identity, susidiarity and all the rest of it, which he professes to defend everywhere else?

As it happens, Major made a fairly long speech on the subject to the Ayrshire Chamber of Commerce on 1 June 1992 when he was no longer subject to the constraints of an imminent election.[51] Perhaps we should look at that in some detail. He begins with a long eulogy of British membership of the European Community, which, he says, underlies the prospects of economic growth in Scotland. Our interests, he argues on familiar lines, are best served as 'part of a United Kingdom that carries weight and authority across Europe'. (What do the other member states think of claims of that kind?) He says of Scotland: 'Does this proud nation really want to be relegated from the heart of Europe, to, at best, its outer fringe?' He seems to have abandoned the dishonest argument that an independent Scotland would have to reapply for membership.

Now, of course, we have discussed all this before. At present, as an invisible country, we are more than 'relegated'; we do not exist. Independence would bring us back into the mainstream. Any 'proud nation' wants to have its own voice in the world, not to be represented by another, even if it is powerful and influential. It is very doubtful, in any case, if the UK can make such a claim in Europe, where it is so often the odd man out and a nuisance. Even in this speech Major boasts about his refusal to agree to the Social Chapter at Maastricht. An independent Scotland, with our European and international instincts, would be a comfortable partner in Europe possibly more so than England which is so often obsessed with its 'weight and authority'. Even alone, we could look after our own interests better than anyone else is likely to do it for us; but with the admission of other small northern countries, we should probably find that we have natural allies on most issues. Together, we should have more votes than the 10 which the UK has at present and of which they make so much fuss.

But unless you are prepared to believe that the UK is motivated only by a desire to be kind and helpful to us (and that would be something new) none of this argument begins to explain why England wants to keep us in the Union. To put it bluntly, what do they get out of it? In fact, Major has a passage in his speech which has a bearing on this point. After referring to 'separatism', as he prefers to call our independence, he continues with this very remarkable paragraph:

But it is not just in Europe that our influence would suffer. Britain's special authority in the United Nations would end. Britain's influence in the Commonwealth would be weakened. Britain's voice in the great world debates on the environment, trade and debt would be stilled.

At first sight, this is hysterical nonsense. Perhaps it is intended to flatter a Scottish audience by pretending that we have such a decisive influence on the standing of the UK; but even as flattery it is unconvincing because it is so exaggerated that no one could take it seriously. The population of Scotland is 5.1 million out of a UK total of 57.4. Would the reduction of the UK population by about 10% have anything like these consequences? I take them in reverse order. There is certainly no reason to suppose that it would have any affect on the right to contribute to the 'world debate', or on influence, such as it is, within the Commonwealth. 'Special authority' in the United Nations means permanent membership and right of veto in the Security Council. This is due to history and might now be justified by the possession of nuclear weapons. It is certainly anachronistic and vulnerable, but it does not depend on population. Weighted voting in the European Community, however, does depend roughly on population and here there is some substance in Major's remark. A reduction by 5.1 million would bring the population of the rest of the UK to well below Germany (62.7) and a little below Italy (57.6)

and France (56.3). It would still be above Spain (38.9).
There might therefore be a move to reduce the vote of the
rest of the UK from 10 to 9; but this is unlikely because it
would require the unanimous agreement of the member
states and it would not be worth while making a fuss over so
small a change.

Is this passage in Major's speech nothing more than
meaningless bluster, like so many of the Conservative
contributions to the constitutional debate? I think that it
does reveal the Conservative obsession with British 'weight
and authority', which is anachronistic in the modern world.
They are desperate to cling to the remnants of their 'great
power' status. It is this which explains so many of their
policies which otherwise seem completely irrational. The
outstanding example is the stubborn and costly addiction to
the Trident submarines long after they have lost any con-
ceivable strategic purpose. They are vastly expensive, dangerous and useless; but they are the last remnant of the
power and glory of the past and do give a shadow of an
excuse for clinging to the permanent seat in the Security
Council. France, which is equally nostalgic for past glory,
behaves in the same way.

Scotland has no patience with this attitude, but we are
involved in it whether we like it or not. I think is the real
explanation why Major is so desperate, by his own admission, to hold on to the Union. The British government, with
remarkable brass neck and self-confidence, has spent bil-
lions of pounds building the base for Trident at Faslane on
the Clyde, in dangerous proximity to the major centre of the
population of Scotland. Scottish independence would
present Major with a very difficult problem. Not only would
the abandonment of Faslane mean a great loss of money, it
would take years to build another base; and where would he
find a site in England that would not be fiercely resisted by
the local people? Wolfe's attitude to the expendable natives
has its modern equivalents.

Of course, there is also the little matter of the tax revenues from the oil in Scottish waters. In the years of Conservative government they have amounted to about £100 billion, or £20,000 for every inhabitant of Scotland. It is because the real reasons why the Conservatives want to keep the Union are of a kind which they cannot admit in public that they have to fall back on trumped-up arguments which are so far-fetched and irrational.

SF I think that my conclusion from all this discussion is that the Scots have allowed themselves to be tricked and conned into maintaining a constitutional arrangement which is harmful to their own interests, not for any good reasons, but to serve an out of date English illusion. We should take a firm decision now to reject it at the first opportunity and emerge into the modern world.

PHS Yes. The Conservatives cling to the hope that the very modest increase in their vote in Scotland in the last election (1.7% compared to an increase in the SNP vote of 7.5%) somehow miraculously means that the constitutional issue will go away. Some of them are more realistic. Lord MacKay of Ardbrecknish, a former Conservative minister in the Scottish Office who was until fairly recently the Chief Executive of the Scottish Conservatives, gave a speech on the matter on 11 July 1992.[52] He pointed out that if a few thousand people had voted differently the Conservatives could have lost all their seats in Scotland. He continued: '11 out of 72 seats and 25.7% of the vote remains a poor position for the governing party and a serious position for the party of the Union. It has to be recognised that there is a Scottish dimension. That dimension has its components in a feeling of unease about the part Scotland plays in the Union, about the way Scotland is treated by the Union, and in particular about the methods which Scottish interests and concerns are dealt with by the Union'.

Lord MacKay's solution, in accordance with his party line, is that the government of Scotland should be improved 'short of setting up a parliament and government', in other words, short of the measures which are needed. The government hopes once again to confuse and divide us with a few minor or symbolic concessions, the equivalent of persuading the natives to sell their country for a few beads and trinkets. We may have been gullible in the past, but I think enough of us now understand the realities to doom any such policy to failure.

The British government have refused a multi-option referendum between the options of status quo, devolution and independence, an admission in itself of their lack of confidence. We may find a way of carrying one through without their approval. What is certain, I think, is that the Scottish people will soon decide that Scotland must cease to be the permanent exception and return to normality as a member state of the European Community with the same rights as any other. We have only to make that decision clear for it to succeed.

NOTES ON FURTHER READING

Classical texts:
There are four classical texts on this subject which, in my view, are essential reading. The three older ones have been reprinted many times, but the following are the most recent editions: *The Declaration of Arbroath* (1320) edited by Sir James Fergusson, with Latin text, translation and introduction (Edinburgh University Press, 1970). *An Account of a Conversation Concerning a Right Regulation of Governments for the Common Good of Mankind* by Andrew Fletcher of Saltoun (1704) in *Fletcher of Saltoun: Selected Writings* edited by David Daiches (Scottish Academic Press, 1979). *The Letters of Malachi Malagrowther* by Sir Walter Scott (1826) edited by Paul H. Scott (Blackwood's, 1981).

The modern classic is *A Claim of Right for Scotland*, the report of the Constitutional Steering Committee, largely drafted by Jim Ross, which was published in July 1988. The text is reprinted, with supporting essays, in a volume with the same title edited by Owen Dudley Edwards (Polygon, 1989).

Commentaries:
The following are a selection: Eric Linklater, *The Lion and the Unicorn* (London, 1935); H.J. Paton, *The Claim of Scotland* (London, 1968); H.J. Hanham, *Scottish Nationalism* (London, 1969); Neil MacCormick, (ed.) *The Scottish Debate* (Oxford, 1970; Michael Hechter, *Internal Colonialism* (London, 1975); Christopher Harvie, *Scotland and Nationalism* (London, 1977); Tom Nairn, *The Break-Up of Britain* (London, 1977 and 1981); Jack Brand, *The National Movement in Scotland* (London, 1978); Craig Beveridge and Ronald Turnbull, *The Eclipse of Scottish Culture* (Edinburgh, 1989; Tom Gallacher, (ed.) *Nationalism in the Nineties* (Edinburgh, 1991); Paul H. Scott, *Towards Independence* (Edinburgh, 1991); William McIlvanney, *Surviving the Shipwreck* (Edinburgh, 1991).

George Rosie's *Scotching the Myth* (1992) and the other papers published by the Scottish Centre for Economic and Social Research (17 Maiden Street, Peterhead, AB 42 6EE) are very useful.

History:

The best, and most recent, one-volume history as a general introduction is Michael Lynch's *Scotland: A New History* (Century, 1991). For the background to the Union there is William Ferguson's *Scotland's Relations with England: A Survey to 1707* (John Donald, 1977) and for an account of the more immediate circumstances, Paul H. Scott's *Andrew Fletcher and the Treaty of Union* (John Donald, 1992).

REFERENCES

1. John Major, Scottish Conservative and Unionist Central Office news release, JS/975/92 of 22 February 1992, pp 10–11.
2. Ian Lang, as 1 above, JS/905/91 of 29 November 1991, p 2.
3. John Major, as 1 above, p 11.
4. Jonathan Swift, *A Short View of the State of Ireland* (1728), Nonesuch Edition, London, 1934, p 507.
5. David McCrone, *Understanding Scotland: The Sociology of a Stateless Nation*, London, 1922, p 133.
6. Owen Dudley Edwards ed., *A Claim of Right for Scotland: Report of the Constitutional Steering Committee* (Edinburgh, 1988), Polygon Determination Series, Edinburgh, 1989, p 14.
7. Eric Linklater, *The Lion and the Unicorn: What England Has Meant to Scotland*, London, 1935, p 26.
8. Allan Massie, 'The Politics of Make-Believe', in *Scotland on Sunday*, 10 May 1992.
9. Lord Home of the Hirsel, letter in the *Scotsman*, 18 May 1992.
10. Sir Walter Scott, *The Letters of Malachi Malagrowther* (1826), ed. P.H. Scott, Edinburgh, 1981, p 10.
11. As 10 above, p 136.
12. Michael Lynch, *Scotland: A New History*, London, 1991, p xiv.
13. Andrew Fletcher of Saltoun, *An Account of a Conversation Concerning a Right Regulation of Governments for the Common Good of Mankind* (1704) in David Daiches ed. *Fletcher of Saltoun: Selected Writings*, Scottish Academic Press, Edinburgh, 1979, pp 136, 114.
14. Edwin Muir, *Scottish Journey*, Edinburgh, 1979, pp 3, 25, 29.
15. As 12 above, pp xx–xxi.
16. Ian Lang, closing speech in 'The *Scotsman* Debate', Usher Hall, Edinburgh, 18 January 1992. (From a recording of the debate.)
17. John MacQueen, *Progress and Poetry: The Enlightenment and cottish Literature*, Edinburgh, 1982, p 5.
18. E.F. Schumacher, *Small is Beautiful*, London, 1974, p 60.

19. Hugh MacDiarmid, 'Direadh', in *Complete Poems*, ed. Michael Grieve and W.R. Aitken, London, 1978, vol II, p 1170.

20. *The Community in 1992*, Office for Official Publications of the European Community, 1987.

21. *Government Expenditure and Revenues in Scotland*, The Scottish Office, 9 March 1992.

22. George Rosie, in *Scotching the Myth*, paper published by the Scottish Centre for Economic and Social Research, 17 Maiden Street, Peterhead.

23. As 22 above.

24. *Scotland on Sunday*, 2 February 1992.

25. Colin Kirkwood, *Vulgar Eloquence*, Edinburgh, 1990, p 343.

26. Ian Lang, news release as 1 above, JS/852/91 of 8 July 1991.

27. Emile Noel, *Scotland on Sunday*, 5 March 1989; the *Scotsman*, 12 June 1989.

28. Lord Mackenzie-Stuart, *Scotland on Sunday*, 8 March 1992.

29. Eamonn Gallagher, opinion submitted to the SNP, Brussels, 18 March 1992.

30. Douglas Hurd, speech in Forres, 19 July 1991. (Moray Conservatives).

31. As 30 above.

32. Garret FitzGerald, the *Irish Times*, 13 July 1991.

33. Mary Robinson, interview in the *Scotsman*, 29 June 1992.

34. Allan Massie, the *Scotsman*, 7 February 1992.

35. So called after the constituency of Tam Dalyell MP in the 1970s. During the debate on the Scotland Act he repeatedly argued that after devolution, English members of the British parliament would not be able to discuss or vote on Scottish matters reserved to the Scottish parliament, but that there would be no similar restriction on Scottish members with regard to the same matters in England.

36. Tony Worthington, *Scotland on Sunday*, 31 May 1992.

37. John Biffen, the *Scotsman*, 29 June 1992.

38. As 6 above, pp 13, 14, 52.

39. Peter Alter, *Nationalism*, London, 1989, p 5.

40. Michael Heseltine, the *Herald*; the *Scotsman*, 8 April 1992.

41. Brian Wilson, *New Statesman and Society*, 28 February 1992.

42. Jean McFadden, the *Herald*, 4 April 1992.

43. Joyce McMillan, *Scotland on Sunday*, 2 August 1992.

44. Allan Massie, the *Scotsman*, 7 February 1992.

45. Helen and William Bannerman, quoted in Elizabeth Hay, *Sambo Sahib*, Edinburgh, 1981, p 111.

46. General James Wolfe, quoted in Robert Wright, *Life of Wolfe*, London, 1864, pp 168–9.

47. Tom Nairn, *the Scotsman*, 16 December 1991.

48. As 22 above.

49. Quoted by Joyce McMillan, *Scotland on Sunday*, 24 May 1992.

50. Michael Fry, in *A Claim of Right for Scotland*, as 6 above, p 94.

51. John Major, text of speech issued by his office.

52. Lord MacKay of Ardbrecknish, the *Herald*, 11 July 1992.